Self Love:
The Journey Home

Series Title Page

Also by Leda Mitrofanis

Me. Myself and I

The Human Case of Mistaken Identity

Book 1

Self Love:
The Journey Home

The Human Case of
Mistaken Identity Series

Book 2

Leda Mitrofanis

BALBOA.PRESS

A DIVISION OF HAY HOUSE

Balboa Press books may be ordered through booksellers or by contacting:

Balboa Press
A Division of Hay House
1663 Liberty Drive
Bloomington, IN 47403
www.balboapress.com
844-682-1282

Print information available on the last page.

ISBN: 979-8-7652-5106-5 (sc)
ISBN: 979-8-7652-5107-2 (hc)
ISBN: 979-8-7652-5105-8 (e)

Library of Congress Control Number: 2024907170

Balboa Press rev. date: 04/12/2024

Dedication

This book is dedicated to my son, George.

Your easy-going personality peppered with your

quick wit and humor, keeps me smiling.

Your sheer presence is a teaching.

And

To all of you looking to return home to self-love.

Acknowledgements

Immeasurable thanks to my mentor

Elaine DeGiorgio and Horus

And to my beloved guide, Anthony

My eternal love and gratitude for your

support, guidance, and wisdom

on what it meant to truly love myself.

And our journeys continue...

Contents

Introduction xi
Prologue I xv
Prologue II xvii

Chapter 1   The Fundamentals of Self-Love 1

Self-Love vs. False Ego................................2
False Ego Love 4
Self-Care 9
Self-Love 11
Radical Honesty..12
Acknowledgment and Self-Knowledge 14
Radical Self-Acceptance.............................19
Self-Trust 24
Self-Forgiveness...27
Forgiveness from the Spiritual Perspective ... 31
Unconditional Self-Love.............................33

Chapter 2   Our Inner Child - Wounds and Self-
Perception...35

Our Early Years..38
Spiritual Perspective 39
Inner Child Wounds 45
Message Internalization 51
Valuation..53
Coping Modalities and Defense
Mechanisms 56

A note here on Ancestral/
Generational Traumas 57

Chapter 3   Patterns and Healing............................59

The Progression of Self-Betrayal,
Guilt/Shame, Self-Punishment, and
Self-Sabotage.. 63
Self-Protection 68
Healing Patterns - Observation and
Discernment – Bearing Witness
Technique 70
Spiritual Perspective on Shadow Healing ...73

Chapter 4   Learning Unconditional Self-Love 77

Accessing our Spiritual Identity/
Divine Self...81
The State of Neutrality...............................83

Chapter 5   More Strategies to Help you Along............85

Epilogue 93
Preamble on Book Three in the Human Case of
   Mistaken Identity Series 95

Introduction

Self-love, the hardest thing you'll ever have to do and yet the most innately natural process we already possess.

I had been procrastinating writing this book as it brought up all my own experiences on this path; causing me to look even deeper at where I still did not love and accept myself. I'm not going to sugar-coat this, it's a painful journey because it requires deeply examining our own wounds and shadows, everywhere we continue to hurt and crucify ourselves, everywhere we keep ourselves in our self-sabotaging behaviors, our own hell-loop of sorts, if you will. Looking at these parts of ourselves, let alone fully accepting and loving them unconditionally is not work for the faint-hearted, which is the reason most people avoid it.

It always seems easier to stay in our comfort zone, even if that zone is not serving us, than to enter in to healing our closed off wounds. As such, most people stick to living and skating on the surface of life...occupying themselves only with the material world and day to day living.

Life, however, has a different plan for us. It brings us people, circumstances, and situations, sometimes incrementally, sometimes as a bombardment, that push us to go deeper into ourselves – into our intentions and motivations, our behavior patterns and the beliefs that created them. To reflect and examine them, to observe and discern them and to decide what we wish to hold on to. When we become aware of "how we tick" so to speak, aka "know thyself," it becomes easier for us to make choices that serve our highest self, to set boundaries and live authentically. Our human trinity of mind, body, spirit thus comes into alignment and balance bringing peace and contentment.

These situations and circumstances are not coincidental or random, but "by design" to propel us into our personal growth and evolution. It is not a punishment or judgement. It's an opportunity. An opportunity to observe our own behaviors, actions, and reactions, thought processes, and triggered emotions...so we can discern what is working for us and what isn't. Thereby shedding what is no longer working, and shifting what is, into the next level of our evolution and self-love.

Self-love is a conscious process that at first seems tiresome, difficult, and fraught with despair. When we start a new diet or workout program, we are usually uncomfortable in the beginning until our body begins to acclimate. The same goes for our emotional body. You're learning what appears to be a new language but in fact is a remembering of what you have forgotten. That is the silver lining. You already know innately how to love yourself; you carry that wisdom from your spiritual origin (see Book 1 - Me, Myself and I). In the human world of social conditioning and ego, you have forgotten. This book is your guide as you journey back home to that love as it was intended and "is."

Walk with me,

Leda

3/19/2024

Prologue I

Who am I? Who am I?

A question that plagued me most of my life. I was born into a specific racial, cultural, and ethnic identity that taught me what to believe, how to think and how to behave. But somewhere beyond this, even as a child, I knew there was more...that I was more; a person, within the external person that everyone saw. A person who did not always agree with what she was told she was, or should be, or had to be. That internal person was silenced more and more as she grew up and became everything her parents, culture and society wanted her to be. But inside she was lost, dying, her sense of self crowded out by the external voices and demands. That self was not allowed to breathe for fear of rejection, abandonment, judgement, and criticism. It was constantly squashed causing excruciating emotional pain, because there is no pain greater than that of separation from the self. That pain and that separation appeared to have obliterated the light of self-love. But this was an illusion, for as I looked for my true self, I discovered it was there all along buried beneath the layers of human conditioning. To my surprise and later realization, it was this very pain, this distress signal, that brought me back to my own self-love.

Prologue II

My Heart

"This morning, I had a vision of my heart. It was round, large, vibrant red, and healthy looking but it had many raised holes that were protruding out of it. It made me sad, and I thought: look at all those holes in my heart fraught from so many traumas and painful experiences…pierced and wounded from all my broken-hearted moments. I truly thought I had a broken heart, indeed, that *I was broken*…that all those hurts and pains had diminished all the love that once lived in my heart. Where had my love gone? Where had I gone?

But when I looked closer, I realized that those "holes" were not holes at all, but vents stemming out from the center of my heart and they were releasing love, compassion, empathy, transparency from its every direction. I came to see that they symbolized instead what a wonderful "open heart" I had. I saw that an open heart is invariably also a heart that was once broken, pierced by wounds that only caused it to open that much more revealing all the love that innately still resided there, even if it was covered up by a wall of self-protection. Each experience lived, overcome, and healed had opened another vent and boy, were there a lot!

In that moment I recognized the beautiful resiliency of my heart and the love it carried. Despite being a never-ending work in progress, I decided to take this love and allow it to teach me what I had forgotten...how to love myself...unconditionally."

CHAPTER 1

The Fundamentals of Self-Love

My clients explore the concept of love quite often as they realize that everything in their life comes down to this. The love I speak of is "self-love." Not to be mistaken for false ego validation. Truly loving ourselves translates into the action of looking at our behaviors, belief systems and shadows with responsibility and accountability. Then integrating the shadow part of ourselves with compassion, empathy, and forgiveness. At this juncture full acceptance is born, acting as the liberating agent which allows us to create the life (relationships, adventures, passions, and missions) that makes our heart and soul sing with unprecedented joy.

Self-Love vs. False Ego

Really, what is self-love? How do we learn truly to love ourselves when we carry so many wounds and emotional damage, sorrow, pains, disappointments, and disillusionments from lifetime to lifetime? How does our soul heal? From where does it get respite and what is the path to healing? Do we ever get to healing, or do we just live this cycle over and over until we break? From where do we source our self-love? And why, why do we so profoundly lack self-love?

Lots of questions that require tangible answers.

The term self-love is bantered around a lot these days as if it was a new buzz word or trend. However, it is neither and is rarely defined with clarity therefore left open to interpretation. This leads to many using the term interchangeably with self-care and confusing it with false ego love. So, let's clarify first, so we may then understand the components of authentic self-love.

I can tell you what self-love is not; it is not false ego love where you pump yourself up with attributes you don't possess and don't truly believe you have. It is not convincing yourself that you are your self-created idealized self-image. Nor is it giving false lip service to yourself and others portraying a false persona that does not exist. Self-love derives from an inner space of authenticity, radical honesty, self-knowledge and acknowledgment, radical and unconditional self-acceptance, self-trust, and self-forgiveness. It is the way in which we perceive, value and honor ourselves despite our faults and shortcomings. It also predicates and encompasses the understanding of your spiritual origins and identity. In short, that you are spiritual being having a temporary physical human existence and not the other way around and what this means tangibly. (See Book 1 – Me, Myself and I)

False Ego Love

As previously defined in Book 1 (Me, Myself and I), our understanding of the ego is broken down as such: true self, ego, and the false ego. Our true self is our eternal spiritual being, the epicenter and total sum of everything we are. Our ego is our existence as a unique individual human being that is aware of both our identities (human and spiritual) and acts as our gatekeeper. Our false ego is when we identify only with our human identity/body and material existence. It's based on the one-dimensional concept we create about ourselves during our lifetime. It contains our shadow side and lies hidden just beneath the ego.

The ego is the crossroad between our true self and the false ego. It resides in our mind and can be healthy, serving the true self or unhealthy, serving the false ego. The ego is in a constant state of calibrating which state to follow: the true self or false ego. This is where we activate our free will choices. What will we choose in any given moment? Have we mastered integration or is one stronger, and directing our life?

All of us, without exception, know how this dynamic plays out in our lives. Our false ego with its inaccurate composite of the self, derived from our woundings, traumas and emotional damage, will continue to self-sabotage our life via repeated destructive patterns until we take notice and begin to unravel what is happening. The process of digging out these *shadowed* wounds is to heal and release them so balance may be restored. The patterns may include the running amok of negative behaviors (greed, jealousy, pride, resentment, selfishness etc.), a self-appointed grandiosity and prestige, constant need for adoration and validation, to name a few. When allowed to run wild for too long, we will eventually believe the false tale it tells us about ourselves. This becomes our self-image. It will steer us far from our true self down into a rabbit hole of self-destruction if we do not pay attention and re-calibrate.

In short, the false ego is the part of us that identifies **only** with our **own** human identity and existence to the exclusion of our true self and those around us.

False ego love says: "to love myself means I have to put myself first at all times, regardless, if that hurts, offends, or diminishes anyone else". It's a "me first" mentality that borders on and can include degrees of selfishness, narcissism, and other ego-centric behavior. Falso ego love has no boundaries and violates those of others in the name of its agenda. This selfishness, camouflaged as self-love, is simply for the gratification and validation of our false self and the demonstration of such to others. It is not true self-love. Selfish individuals do not recognize love within themselves and thereby look to get it from others. They look to others from the perspective of "what they can get, what's in it for them" mentality. There is no sense of giving, only taking, perceiving others' existence only in terms of what they have to offer them. Their relationships are all transactional and not based on love. They cannot understand connection because they cannot see it or connect with themselves. They are simply constantly trying to fill the void within them of where love should be.

False ego love is only interested in the physical level of self-love and completely bypasses the mental and emotional state as it does not wish to acknowledge, address, or do the inner work to heal any wounds. It stays squarely on the surface of life skating through on a superficial level. It will also try at all costs to sabotage and discourage you from any activity that would initiate personal growth, healing, and evolution. For its existence and identity is reliant on you staying "stuck". It is the part of you that is wounded and does not want to face the pain. It will instead create a false persona, called your idealized self-image, to keep you in avoidance.

As you can see this is not authentic self-love. It is important to note that unfortunately, our society is filled with those who are locked into their false ego, who intentionally mislead, whose charm and gift of gab make us believe in something that is merely an illusion, those who take advantage of our vulnerabilities and our weaknesses for their own gratification and use. As a society we are becoming more and more enamored with excessive financial wealth, physical appearance, status, position, fame, and titles at the expense of honesty, loyalty, dignity, integrity, and self-respect. There are those who will forfeit everything and anything to attain these outer status symbols at the expense of losing and continuing to sell out their true sense of self and further stray from their own self-love. They will appear to say and do all the right things, mimicking true substance and authenticity inordinately well because at some point they have begun to believe their own illusion, their idealized self-image.. Do not fall prey to this. Every single one of us has been gifted with discernment. It is crucial that we learn to always exercise it. Stay in observation, discern with compassion, and remember, these are just wounded individuals that need a guiding light to come back home to their authentic selves. The more you love yourself the brighter a light you are by your mere existence and lead by example.

Self-Care

Self-care is a natural extension of self-love but not the primary foundation of self-love. Many of us believe that practicing self-care is all that is needed to define self-love. This is not so. Self-care is part of self-love but not the whole and is most often practiced when self-love to some degree is already present. Self-care must be coupled with inner emotional work and the other components of self-love.

Self-care can be exercised at the physical level and the mental and emotional level. On the physical level, as most of us already know, it includes a healthy clean diet, daily exercise, adequate sleep, and good grooming and hygienic habits. It also includes regular medical preventive care such as physical checkups and frequent therapeutic body work such as massages, Reiki healing and the like.

On the mental level, self-care includes setting healthy boundaries and honoring them, time management skills that create overall well-being and balance, positive self-talk, visioning and goal setting, and a solid working decision-making process which includes observation and discernment. Here we also include various psychotherapies when needed and medication only if absolutely necessary.

On the emotional level, self-care includes acknowledgement of various emotions from a point of neutrality to foster clarity and accuracy, stabilizing emotions via any of the following methods - breath work, meditation, journaling, exercising or solo sport, dance/art/music, crafting/cooking/gardening, spending time in nature or any other solo activity which immerses your attention 100%. Additionally, any emotional therapeutic modalities and therapies.

On the spiritual level, self-care includes a religious or spiritual practice and/or participation in communities of such. Quiet moments of self-reflection and/or meditation focused on your divine self and divine source.

Remember, self-care is often confused for complete self-love when it is only one component and an outward demonstration of self-love. Let's keep going.

Self-Love

Self-love requires radical honesty, radical and unconditional self-acceptance, acknowledgment and self-knowledge, self-trust, self-forgiveness, and unconditional self-love. Without these, self-love is nothing more than false ego love with a partial dose of self-care. When self-love grows, the false ego love will grow silent automatically, and self-care will increase as a by-product.

Now we can breakdown the components of self-love.

Can you be totally honest with yourself about yourself? Can you identify your shortcomings? Moments when you knew you were out of line but did it anyway? The behaviors and beliefs you have enacted that did not serve you well. Behaviors such as lying, cheating, controlling, manipulation, deception, stealing, verbal attack or abuse, physical attack or abuse, self-destructive behaviors and patterns, self-punishment, condescending, dismissive, jealous etc. - You get the idea. Can you acknowledge these behaviors and forgive yourself?

Radical Honesty

Radical honesty is the first step in the self-love process. It necessitates that you tell yourself the truth, the whole truth and nothing but the truth, no matter how bad it is, to yourself about yourself. You don't need to share it with anyone else, although at some point during your healing you will find you will, to assist you. The point being, you must recognize and bring into your awareness all parts of you. All your shortcomings, wounds, dysfunctional family history, missteps, and bad behaviors. The positive ones can be just as challenging as the negative ones. As some people have difficulty acknowledging their intelligence, kindness, generosity, success etc. because they have been taught and conditioned to play small and diminish themselves in the name of humility and humbleness. Stating who and what you are without filter and from a state of *neutrality*, both negatively and positively, constitutes radical honesty.

This can seem a monumental task and it is very difficult, painful, and challenging at times because it brings to the surface suppressed wounds that have been buried. It also brings to the surface the shadows parts of your personality you have disowned in the name of your self-protection. Those buried places within us that are hiding our pain, shame, and guilt – that lead us to behave and act out from our wounds. When we live from our wounded self, Life inevitably shows us where we are bleeding. It's Life's way of showing us where we have been cut and never healed. Facing our wounds is a tremendous act of courage that allows us to integrate the shadows and all their behavior patterns, bringing us back into wholeness and out of fragmentation. In the wholeness we find balance, peace, love, and happiness. As difficult as shadow work is, it's also the road to healing and the wounded eventually becomes the healer. We will talk more in depth about this in the chapter on Inner Child Wounds.

Acknowledgment and Self-Knowledge

"Know thyself" the famous quote of Ancient Greek philosophers and Lao Tzu's "Knowing others is wisdom, knowing yourself is enlightenment" speaks directly across time, that the way forward to unconditional self-acceptance and ultimately self-love begins with acknowledgement and self-knowledge. We cannot accept what we are unaware of.

The first step in the 12 Step program is admitting your addiction and it is noted as being the hardest step. Likewise, noticing and acknowledging that there is a wound or pattern that you need to address is difficult, but it too is the first step that must be made. Our soul knows exactly how to make us aware of what needs to be looked at. It is the subtle feeling of dissatisfaction that enters your awareness and causes you to turn right instead of left at the crossroad. That underlying nudge that something is not working, that you are not feeling fulfilled, that something is missing despite all your external circumstances telling you otherwise. That is the feeling you shouldn't ignore. You need to hone-in on it like a radar that picked up an SOS signal. Because it is in fact an SOS signal. Your soul is sending you a message that all is not well. That somewhere you are disowning yourself, hiding or lying or giving yourself away.

The first step is to acknowledge the signal. Don't be afraid of it, don't ignore it, don't suppress it, or cast it aside for later. Take it out into the light and shake it out like you would dust from a rug. You don't have to analyze it, just bring it into your conscious awareness and sit with it. In a very short time, it will make itself fully known to you and show you what you need to do.

This might sound counterintuitive, but it is in fact the key to the process. Your true or authentic self is not something you find or go looking for. It is not something you have to create or conjure up. It already exists; albeit hidden, cloaked, masked, cast aside, or buried., but it absolutely exists. It's a matter of you calling it forward and allowing it to "be", to co-exist with you, as you, without judgement or fear. The tap on your shoulder is a clue that something is awry and needs to be looked at closely. Many times, we are "aware" that something is off but do not "acknowledge it," consciously. This is because we are afraid and not yet ready to. Awareness and acknowledgment are not the same thing. Acknowledgment is an affirmative action that leads to self-knowledge.

Self-knowledge breaks out into a few components. This is simply because most of us operate in three parts (as noted earlier); the part of yourself you believe you are in any given moment (ego), the part of yourself you want everyone else to believe you are (false ego), and who you really are (true self - the authentic you). Confusing? It can be when it's laid out this way. However, most of us function this way subconsciously all the time and don't even realize it. We shift from one to the other effortlessly depending on where we're at, at any given time and with whom. Ask yourself; have you ever behaved differently when you're at home with your partner and family than you do at work? What about close friend's vs acquaintances? Or how about with a romantic interest vs the community you participate in? We shift personas all the time and we have come to accept this back and forth as "normal" because after all not everyone in your life carries the same importance, right? And while this may be true, your personality and authenticity should be the same throughout any interaction or in any situation.

Self-knowledge is defined as knowing where you are in this paradigm at any given moment. To become aware consciously when you are shifting and altering your behavior and who you are, according to where and with whom you are. Paying attention to where we are being inauthentic is the best roadmap to what underlying beliefs we are holding onto that are not working for us.

Do not confuse what you disclose about yourself with authenticity. Spilling your private affairs to everyone you meet is not being authentic, it's oversharing where it's not appropriate or warranted. Being authentic means your essential character has a stable consistent alignment with who you truly are without the fears of rejection, abandonment, judgement, or criticism which most often is the culprit to our constant shifting and creating personas that do not resonate with us. In our desire to be liked, popular and loved we shift our behaviors and personality traits constantly to accommodate and please those around us to secure this validation. Some of us create an entirely false persona, a mask if you will to the outer world. We believe this mask will hide our perceived flaws and short-comings and allows us to present ourselves to the outer world the way we *wish* to be perceived. This is our idealized self-image. The extreme physical manifestation of this is social media which has become the ultimate marketing tool of self-branding. Many portray lives they wish they had, but don't, while others portray physical attributes that don't exist or achievements that never came to pass. Why is this? Because we are afraid if we show our authentic truth, it will not be good enough...*we* won't be good enough.

Start paying attention to the patterns showing up in your life. It reads as the same play over and over but with different characters. This is a telltale sign. Observe yourself and be radically honest about what you see. With this we move into radical self-acceptance.

Radical Self-Acceptance

Radical self-acceptance comes up next and predicates that you have first worked on acknowledgment/self-knowledge and are practicing and mastering radical honesty. Again, you cannot accept what you are unaware of. Uncovering the many levels of our patterns and behaviors takes time and is incremental because they are often shrouded and painful. It may prompt memories and moments wherein you feel you are re-living wounds and circumstances that hurt you. Although difficult or challenging it is necessary to feel these wounds as a form of emotional release both from the emotional body as well as the physical and mental. Harboring painful moments causes suppression. This energy needs somewhere to go, and when not released often manifests as physical and/or mental illness. The key is to dig out from where the pattern or behavior originated so that it may be released. Once release takes place then you can begin to work on acceptance.

Can you love yourself despite your shortcomings, perceived weaknesses, or limitations? Can you accept yourself despite all of these, knowing that they may be part of your social conditioning and/or response to your social conditioning and originated most likely from your early childhood?

Self-acceptance seems very challenging to most of us, simply because we are socially conditioned to spend most of our time "fixing" what we perceive is wrong with us. We spend much more time on self-criticism and comparison than we do on loving ourselves as we are, with compassion and empathy. We are taught from very young that we are imperfect beings, sinners, unworthy and other such monikers from our culture and religious beliefs and that we must rely on a form of mercy, grace, or repentance to be made whole. But what if you knew and were taught that you were born "perfect", that there was nothing "to fix", that you were already whole...how would that have altered your life trajectory?

When a small child falls and scrapes a knee, they begin to cry and automatically look to their parents for how to respond to the fall. Yes, the physical pain is there for a short bit, and they will cry, but their *perception* of the fall comes from the parent. If the parent kisses the "boo-boo" and relays the perspective, in both word and demeanor, that the fall is minor, then the child will perceive it that way as well, stop crying fairly quickly and go back to playing. If, on the other hand, the parent reacts in a way that the fall is akin to a catastrophe, again both in word and demeanor, then the child cries harder and longer, perhaps has a meltdown, and most probably will not return to playing. In each instance, the parents' reaction dictates what is *imprinted* on the child. This imprint becomes the child's reality beginning the formation of their coping skills. Furthermore, if the parent scolds the child for falling conveying the message that the child is at fault and compounds it with labels such as: you always fall, you never pay attention, you're clumsy, you're always causing a problem etc. this affects how a child begins to perceive him/herself. Here is where their self-perception takes form.

In the same way, if we are taught that we are imperfect simply because we are born, that it's a lifetime affliction, that it's irreversible and constantly needs to be fixed, then guess what, this becomes our *imprinting,* and we don't learn to accept ourselves. Instead, we stay locked in a lifetime of struggle trying to score brownie points with others, the Divine, and ourselves, constantly attempting to prove we are good enough. How is this enlightening and conducive to personal and spiritual growth? These teachings undermine and diminish the truth of our spiritual nature and light that as small children we innately know ourselves to be (more on this in Chapter 2).

The key to self-acceptance is to unravel everything you have ever been taught. Sort through it and decide if what you've been told resonates with you or not. Was it handed to you, or did you decide this was your truth from your own volition and experiences? This process is a lifelong practice and will come into play as situations arise. As you do the work to unravel and discern your belief systems, your behaviors will shift as a result, especially those that are no longer serving you, and your self-acceptance barometer will automatically rise. You will begin to embrace all of yourself and the process.

Self-Trust

Self-trust goes hand in hand with self-acceptance. But let's go back for a moment. What does it mean to trust yourself? Are you always doubting your decisions, choices, and intuition? Do your coping skills require the need for you to always consult someone else for guidance or input when faced with a situation or crises? Are you looking for someone else or a horoscope et al to tell you who you are and where you're going or how to "fix" yourself? Do you give your power away to others just to be appeasing or conversely to receive validation?

Building self-trust starts in early childhood with our parents/caregivers. They are the ones who teach us and navigate our self-perception by helping and allowing us from early on to learn the skills of observation, discernment, self-assessment, and critical thinking coupled with resiliency. (More on this in Chapter 2). As we grow up, our daily life presents us with many situations, people and circumstances designed to hone and solidify our self- trust. The more we know and trust ourselves the more self-confidence we will feel and exude.

Self-trust begins when we learn to give ourselves permission to do the things that honor our inner self and being. Permission to engage in the activities that feed us inwardly. Not in a selfish way but in a way that brings us into balance with the outer world and its demands. When we do this, we are in effect listening to and feeding our soul. The more we honor our inner voice the more we return to a place where we realize that our sense of value and worth stem from within us and not our successes and achievements as defined by the outer world. When our sense of value and worth is exercised in this way, we begin to feel more at peace, safer in the world and more accepting of who we are. And when these three conditions: peace, safety and self-acceptance expand within us the more we learn to trust ourselves and this eventually becomes our new way of living. As your trust in yourself continues to grow, you will become more comfortable in expressing your authenticity. This is the outer manifestation of self-acceptance.

When your self-trust solidifies within you it means that you trust that *you* will know best what is "right" for you in a particular moment. It means you know yourself well enough to know what you need, what you want, how you respond and what your limitations are. It means knowing you are on the right path for your development and life and not comparing it to others. Self-trust builds and requires a strong sense of self, i.e., knowing your true identity (Book 1), your inherent value and core beliefs, embracing your authenticity and living it as a daily practice. It means that you do not second guess your intuition, because you know without a doubt it is your direct link to your inner wisdom and compass and Divine source. Staying close to core values such as: integrity, responsibility and accountability, compassion, and forgiveness, learning from your experiences and applying it, and self-respect and equanimity all help with strengthening your self-trust.

Self-Forgiveness

There is no self-love without self-forgiveness. We are spiritual beings having a temporary physical existence. Our human existence is fraught with experiences that teach us lessons to propel our personal and spiritual growth. Part of these experiences is making mistakes. All of us without exception have moments when we wished we didn't say something, or do something, that we could have done differently in hindsight. We either feel remorse or contrition that we have hurt someone else and consequently ourselves or we remain stubborn in our being "right" rather than being in "self-love." It is crucial to understand here that this is an inevitable part of the learning process. What is key is how we handle the mistakes and errors we've made and those that were made towards us.

Many a times we refuse to forgive because we feel it is a sign of weakness or that by forgiving another's hurtful action, we are somehow condoning the behavior thus allowing it to continue (this is in effect a boundary issue). In other instances, forgiveness is felt to be a moral or religious imperative thus rendering the offended with the feeling that their hurt or pain was somehow invalid or insignificant. Still others feel that forgiveness is not necessary or possible, thereby burying their feelings only to have them resurface later in life when a trigger presents itself.

But quite simply, extending forgiveness to others is something we are in essence doing for ourselves for there is an unseen energy that releases when we forgive, affecting both parties allowing for a sudden lightness to be felt. In contrast, by holding onto anger, resentment, pain or hurt we continue to stay locked in a loop of negativity that does not allow *us* to move forward. It hinders us in gravitating *to us* the positive emotions and experiences we desire to have in our life. Forgiveness is a release that equals freedom. Letting go of the negative emotions frees us internally. We literally free up brain space in which something new can enter, our nervous system is alleviated, our hearts filled with peace instead of internal conflict. Letting go in forgiveness is not an easy task; it takes courage and strength to move beyond human pride and ego. It takes awareness, acknowledgment, radical honesty, responsibility, and accountability. We can practice forgiveness at any time, even if many years or the parties involved have passed. The other person will feel it through a release of energy as noted above.

Forgiveness of the self is the most challenging and the type of forgiveness most of us practice the least. However, it allows for the releasing of any shame and guilt we are holding onto no matter how deeply seeded. Some of us are harder on ourselves than we would be with anyone else. Guilt and shame are heavy burdens to carry. When left unreleased they flat spin and magnify in our consciousness creating an endless internal conflict that deteriorates us slowly. They manifest outwardly as self-punishment and self-sabotage. It is not necessary to crucify ourselves for redemption. This does not bring enlightenment, only self-torment. Understand that healing supersedes redemption.

Self-forgiveness is equally important when someone has committed an offense/hurt to us. Many times, we practice forgiveness towards the offender, and yet continue to hold onto the *imprinting* of what they said or did unconsciously perpetuating the pain and taking it forward with us. For e.g., our parents might have labeled us in a certain way and even though we might not hold it against them, the *imprinting* of that label has stayed, and we continue to live it out as our identity all the while feeling resentment and/or crippled for the manifestation of the label itself and our inability to release it from our psyche. It is very important to discern with awareness and courage if we are doing this to ourselves. Here self-forgiveness is paramount because it is essential you forgive yourself for continuing to burden yourself with a label that is untrue. You have the power to unsaddle yourself from any imprinting. This is an act of deep self-love through self-forgiveness.

Self-forgiveness is an act of healing and ultimate self-love. It is the road to true internal freedom which then ripples outward changing your own life and those of others. It is not a death sentence to make mistakes, it's a death sentence to stay in them over and over, for we continue to hurt ourselves by our own hand.

Now let's go one step further and look at forgiveness from the spiritual perspective, and this predicates that you have read Book 1, on understanding our spiritual identity.

Forgiveness from the Spiritual Perspective

When we look at forgiveness purely from this perspective, we see that it is rendered mute in the face of *understanding*. This is because in spirit we are all "one," there is no separation. The notion of separation is a human illusion. Each one of us is a soul of light incarnated in our respective human lives to evolve and learn from our individual specific life lessons. How each of us does this is unique to us. No-one person is better than another, just different lessons and hence experiences. When we rub-up against each other causing conflict, hurt, pain, betrayal and the like, our human pride and egos come into play making forgiveness challenging at best on the human level. However, the key in this moment is to step into our true spiritual identity and to perceive the other as our fellow innocent soul of light. And instead of plunging into the emotional charge of pain, hurt, guilt or shame, to ask ourselves, what is this moment, this conflict teaching *me*, that I need to look at? *What are we both here to learn, respectively?*

Now... "forgiveness" becomes unnecessary and understanding becomes a tool of the highest order. Now... the lessons can be learned for both parties, without judgement, criticism, hurt, pain, shame, or guilt because you *understand* we are all here, from our spiritual home, working out our own lessons. You don't hold anything against anyone or yourself. Instead of engaging in the blame game or self-condemnation, you become introspective and focus on what the interaction is teaching you on your road of evolution and you shift accordingly. And lastly, this allows you to genuinely release the other person with gratitude and love, wishing them the best on their continued journey and thanking them for the gift of insight you each received, respectively.

This spiritual practice is not easy, but we cannot condemn another or ourselves and claim we love ourselves, for this is spiritual bypassing and not in truth. Look at where you need to practice forgiveness and see if you can instead employ "understanding" from this perspective.

Unconditional Self-Love

To fully embrace and live out unconditional self-love, you must first master all the components as described in this chapter and further become aware of all the parts of yourself – the good, the bad and the ugly. You must learn to accept and integrate all these parts, especially the shadow aspects (the wounds), as you do the inner work to unravel, heal and release them.

No-one can give you more love than you are willing to give yourself. They can try, but you will have the ability to receive and accept only at the level you are currently at. You will subconsciously block the rest, especially if you have shadow beliefs which tell you; "you aren't worthy, or good enough, or deserving." Some or all these core beliefs, which run as a computer program in the background of our life, begin in childhood. Our self-perception and the degree to which we are loved or deemed loveable is created within our nuclear family environment. Embracing unconditional self-love requires us to turn back and look at how our inner child was formed and developed.

Take a breath and let's go.

CHAPTER 2

Our Inner Child - Wounds and Self-Perception

The journey of self-love is not perceived as an easy one because it requires that you love yourself unconditionally; shadows and all. It requires that we go in and look at our wounds and vices (shadows) and slowly bring them out, one by one, into the light so they may be healed. This "shadow work' is not as difficult as you might believe. It only appears so because we have been conditioned to avoid our shadows and the parts of ourselves that we have disowned, feel guilty about or are ashamed of. The parts of ourselves that cause us deep pain, that rock the very core of our being, that tells us we **don't deserve**, or **we're not good enough** or **we're unworthy**. These are the three baseline beliefs that all shadows eventually come down to.

These shadow parts of ourselves begin to form in childhood as we learn to cope to the world around us. Growing up we often repress and suppress them, stuffing them deep into our subconscious where we can pretend, they don't exist. But exist they do, and they create the very coping and defense mechanisms and behaviors we still use as adults. They create the false ego constructs which tell us; worry not, fear not for I will keep you safe…and the ego does so by building a protective wall around us…only for us to realize that this wall is in essence a detrimental illusion keeping out both positive and negative alike along with other emotional side effects. If we were taught as children that looking at our shadow parts without fear is a natural process of healing and release, we would all suffer a great deal less. Nor would we be projecting and deflecting our wounds onto others. You see the shadow part of us is not such a cause of distress in and of itself, it's how we personally *perceive* this shadow part that causes the distress.

I was raised in a family whereas immigrants my parents were very focused on physical survival, especially in my early years, as most immigrants are. The finetuning and nuances of parenthood were not top of mind. They, like most, "parented" by what was handed down to them from their parents, and grandparents before them, and their social-cultural upbringing. All parents do the best they can with the knowledge and state of existence they have at that moment. Some were raised during wars or in impoverished circumstances, while others experienced racial, cultural, or sexual prejudices, still others coped with addictions, sexual, physical and/or verbal abuse, all circumstances in which mere survival is paramount. Others have had a milder form of hardship and/or negligence, yet, all have, in some way, shape or form, been affected by passed down generational traumas and adverse ancestral beliefs.

As such, the psychological effects of their parenting were not always the focal point on their radar. It is important to remember this, as it eliminates any future blame and victimhood. Our parents were once children also and pending what *their* parents experienced and suppressed, it naturally filtered down to them and then was subconsciously bequeathed and imprinted onto you. This is not a life sentence, but merely a structure of understanding how our shadows may come about. We can break this chain and its effects by doing our own shadow work, which has a two-fold result. One, it heals and liberates us emotionally and two, it allows us to parent consciously when and if we become parents or caregivers.

So, let's break it down so we can see how much of this is formed.

Our Early Years

It is in our early years that our self-perception and self-love are formulated. We are naturally born with a sense of our self and self-love - you only need to watch a baby play and their interactions to understand this. They move organically and naturally. But as we grow up observing the actions of the adults around us and being *at the effect* of them, we begin to lose this and start to modify our behavior to survive in our environment.

When do we lose our self-love? When do we stop loving ourselves and why?

Spiritual Perspective

In our very early childhood, we have an innate unconscious expectation to be loved and nurtured. How this expectation is met will determine our self-perception. From the spiritual perspective, when we are physically born into our human identity from our spiritual home (see Book 1), we exist in a state of pure "beingness" and love, and we organically act from this identity because we remember our home as it's still fresh. When children begin to articulate language, we see them often telling their parents, in snippets, of the home they left. But most of the time we dismiss this as nonsensical baby talk. Have you ever seen a baby crawling on the floor and babbling as if they're talking to someone? Or pointing to something where you see nothing? How about the imaginary friend that some children have till 6 or 7yrs old? None of this is imaginary but what they still see and perceive from the home they just left. There is an adaptation phase when we come in from our spiritual dimension to the human one that needs to be met with love, compassion, and spiritual understanding. If we moved to a foreign territory with no knowledge of the language or culture or way of life, would we want to be yelled at, labeled, punished or would we want to be treated with love and compassion, and assisted in adapting to a different way of life?

With each passing year children begin to forget their spiritual home. It slowly becomes a memory as they adapt and cope to their human identity. This can make them sad or frustrated, causing them to meltdown as well. Most parents do not understand this and believe the child is being insubordinate or behaving badly etc. But this is not true. How many times have we heard a young child say "no!" emphatically to something or almost everything? They are not pushing our boundaries to be spiteful and difficult as we have been taught to believe. It's rather amazing that we can believe such a thing to be true! What they are merely trying to say is "this is not how it is or should be." Remember, we need to understand them from *their* perspective, not ours. They are coming from the perspective of the spiritual home they just left, not the human home they have yet to experience. And there are vast differences between the two. And as such, they are, without consciously realizing it, teaching us to remember who we are also – spiritual beings of love – and teaching us what it means to live as spiritual beings of love. Children are spiritual beings of equal value to the adults around them.

I wish to reiterate here what was touched on in Book 1, as it's important to understanding the spiritual role children play in our lives. Part of the "human conditioning" is this concept of labeling. When we begin to saddle our children with labels such as: fat/skinny, smart/dumb, lazy/disciplined, well-behaved/disruptive, good-looking/ average, etc. and most especially; "good/bad," we serve to undermine their own perception of who they are, when they already know who they are! They innately already know they are "perfect, acceptable and loveable." So, is it any wonder they get resistant, frustrated, and angry with this? Labeling children creates the foundation of their human self-perception based on how *we* perceive them as opposed to allowing them to organically discover themselves. When they are labeled in any way, positively or negatively, it becomes an internalized message that they will carry for the rest of their lives, and they will inevitably reflect this message back by beginning to live up to these labels, becoming self-fulfilling prophesies. These labels can create limitations or conversely, unrealistic standards. In both cases the child is struggling with feeling "not good enough." These labels also create an innate sense that something is innately wrong with them and therefore are not loveable as they are and need to be fixed (more on this below). The key is to offer love, affection, guidance, and regulation without the labels. We were once children also so let us ask ourselves: do we remember when we were labeled as a child? How did it make us feel? How did we react? How did it affect our life trajectory?

Children also serve as our faithful mirrors. They observe and internalize our words and behaviors and reflect them back to us. This makes most parents uncomfortable, resistant, or angry especially when they are not flattering. The child hit a nerve without even realizing they were doing so. Then the parents punish the child because *the parent(s)* was triggered. Being "triggered" is an indication that somewhere there is an unconscious false belief in play within the parent(s). What an incredible, teachable moment this is for the parent(s)! Their beloved child is giving them an opportunity to notice, remember and acknowledge a wounded part of themselves, that they have disowned and adopted from their own parents, for the purpose of healing and release. This is not a form of some type of call-out or sass but a subconscious gift they give you to heal yourself, by examining your own childhood labels and returning to your own truth. Everyone benefits when we see these moments and challenges from this perspective.

When we begin to see *ourselves* as spiritual beings, then we will see our children this way as well. We will no longer see them as extensions of our ego or as some form of ownership. When we see them as mutual spiritual beings that come together with us as a family, then our behavior will naturally and automatically reflect this belief as well and we will think twice or refrain from following human societal conventions of labeling, stereotyping, and judging. It is important we give them the freedom to figure out who they are with us as their guiding force even if it wasn't given to us as a child. Be the adult who breaks this chain, for yourself and future generations in your lineage. Children are a wonderful gift that remind us of who we once were and who we presently are by their sheer presence – our divine self, not our human self. And this is why they are our faithful mirrors.

Inner Child Wounds

Now that we have established the circumstances under which we come into our lifetime. We can move into understanding how our childhood wounds are formed, what they are, the shadows they create, and how we take them into adulthood.

With each passing year, children adapt to the social conditioning of their nuclear family and community and eventually to human society at large. Their spiritual home becomes a distant memory and mostly completely forgotten. Disconnection, social conditioning, suppression of the authentic self out of fear are all components of how this happens.

Let's take an example using some common beliefs and using a fictitious person named Eve. She grew up in a family where she was not taught or "reflected" self-love. On the contrary, she was taught to always put others "first" because that would make her "a good selfless person." She was also the youngest and by default this meant in her family that she was the least knowledgeable in the hierarchy, something she was reminded of constantly and she was not given affection freely, rather criticized quite often. So how does all this manifest?

As you can immediately see, constantly putting others first led her to 'giving herself away vs. giving of herself." It also reared some the following subconscious belief systems:

- "Everyone else is more important than me."
- "I don't matter / I am not significant or important."
- "If I chose to do something for myself instead of someone else, I am bad and selfish."

- "I have to please everyone else all the time or be alone."

- "Others only like me when I am giving something to them."

- "I derive my self-worth by how much I give to others."

- "I am only validated by how well I perform this family credo."

- "I am not worthy as I am."

Being considered the least knowledgeable in her family led to:

- "I always need to check with someone else if what I am thinking/doing is right."

- "I always need the approval of someone smarter than me."

- "I'm not smart enough to be a leader, I will always be a follower."

- "My intuition doesn't work, God forgot it when I was born."
- "I can't trust my own judgement."
- "I am not good enough."
- "I have to constantly study and learn new things to show how knowledgeable I am."

Lack of affection and constant criticism led to:

- "I am not loveable."
- "There is something innately wrong with me."
- "I am/was born broken."
- "I am always doing something wrong; I can't do anything right."
- "I'm not good enough."
- "I don't deserve love, success etc."
- "I need to be constantly fixed in all areas of my life."

Belief systems do not develop overnight. They are a gradual process of which we are completely unaware because they become slowly embedded in the subconscious and begin running like a computer program in the background. This program remains in the subconscious as we move into adulthood, running our life choices until circumstances and events begin drawing our attention to them.

Our belief systems shape our behavior and cause an innate insecurity within us to take hold. We begin to adapt and modify our behavior accordingly so we can survive, feel better, fit in, camouflage, protect, hide etc. You get the idea. These developed behaviors inevitably don't serve us very well as they run counter to our spiritual identity and who we truly are. But as we forget our true spiritual identity and who we are at our core, with each passing year, we begin to adopt our human identity as our primary identity complete with all its inaccuracies. We become out of balance and believe who others say we are. We begin living someone else's truth and not our own.

Let's go back to our example. These are some of the possible behaviors that manifest from the above belief systems.

- People-pleasing
- Constant need and seeking external validation by becoming an over-achiever.
- Proving of self-worth – over-shadowing others, being the center of attention, being a know-it-all
- Criticizing or demeaning others to elevate self-worth (also a self-projection)
- Arrogant, Conceited, Self-Important
- *Internal* self-criticism
- Perfectionism and unrealistic high standards for self and others
- Controlling and manipulating circumstances to have needs and insecurities met.

Message Internalization

What's important to note with these behaviors is that they all stem from how we internalized the messages we received as children. The messages are varied and many, depending upon our specific personal childhoods and are always accompanied with "labels" as discussed, earlier. These messages create internal wounds that read as abandonment and rejection which strips away our innocence, beauty, and purity. We become self-conscious, feel guilty and ashamed and so we give our power away. We suppress and hide from others the parts of ourselves that are deemed unacceptable and so put on our mask. Our true self seems to have all but disappeared and we live in a constant state of internal push/pull because at bottom we still have a remembrance of who we are, even if it's a trace. And we have come to call this "normal upbringing."

Why do we find it so difficult to shed our belief systems from our psyche?

First, as young children we cannot distinguish between a behavior and an identity, between "doing" and "being". Doing a bad thing is not the same as being a bad person. When children are admonished "you're a bad boy/girl" they internalize "I am bad" not "I did a bad thing." This internalization diminishes the child's self-worth and value. If the parent instead consciously made the distinction for the child, the child would understand that their self-identity is intact and that their behavior is fluid and a choice that they themselves can modify. Parental guidance now becomes empowering, not disempowering.

Second, in a child's eyes the parent is the ultimate authority. Therefore, if a parent labels a child positively or negatively it will absolutely solidify in the child's psyche. When a parent tells their child they're bad (or any other label), the resulting guilt and/or shame internalized will become the new identity the child will operate from moving forward. This God-like authority that parents have from the child's perspective can easily make a child feel either weak, small, and vulnerable or conversely, if the label is positive, uplifted, empowered and confident. A note on positive labeling: this can work against the child if the parent is over-compensating. Children can feel inauthenticity like a fine-tuned radar and many times will not verbalize this. Therefore, it is crucial that positive messages be delivered with authenticity and not as lip service and further reinforced with action that validates them.

Valuation

Parents reflect a child's value to them by how they treat them. How many times have we seen parents demonstrate more love and approval to the child who is "performing well" according to their beliefs? The child who is easy, funny, good-looking, entertaining, talented, smart, eats well, sleeps well, is never "challenging" in any way etc. Value is **inherent,** not earned. It does not come from what "we do and how well we do it" but from "who we are." When we send the message that our child's value is derived by how they perform or if they attain certain qualities, we undermine their very existence and are teaching them by demonstration that love is **"conditional."** The child then learns to derive their value from outside of themself (externally) giving their power away and will always be at the mercy of circumstances and people, and their life will be a constant roller coaster of self-assessment based on how others treat and perceive them. They begin to live in a constant state of comparison, mood swings and an underlying sense of emotional chaos ensues. Here is where we often see the initial signs of depression creeping in or conversely, the acting out of anger or the onset of addiction depending on the child's coping and defense mechanisms. Self-judgement and self-criticism abound. The isolation, disconnection from self, lack of self-trust and the struggle for self-identity are born. This, if left unaddressed continues into adulthood and may magnify. Value simply exists, it comes from our spiritual self and children inherently already know this. They already know they are complete and whole. When we do not perceive them in this way, we do both them and us a disservice. Note to parents...if you perceive your child as whole and complete, he/she will in turn teach you to see yourself this way. This is the silver lining and the gift they bring you.

A note for those who experienced severe verbal abuse, physical abuse, sexual or otherwise at the hands of the adults whose care they were in. This transgression is severely damaging and a serious human and spiritual violation of the highest accord. But it does not have to be a life sentence. Healing from such trauma is not only possible, but you are the ones who become the guides and healers, the advocates, and life-changers for others. You are not broken, your core-essence - your true identity - your spirit and divine self are always intact regardless of your human circumstances. This knowledge is your superpower and the springboard and strength from which you can reclaim your life and self-identity. Use your divine, spiritual aspect as the guide to your healing (more on this in Chapter 4 & 5).

Coping Modalities and Defense Mechanisms

As we have established, wounds are created within us from our childhood environments regardless of their severity. If we go back to the example at the beginning of the chapter, we can see how the messages Eve received became internalized beliefs, which in turn became behaviors. These behaviors subconsciously formed to serve as measures of self-protection. The pain we feel for not being recognized or seen for who we truly are is a form of **rejection and abandonment of our very essence and being and serves as the foundational core of all wounds.** This is so painful for a child who cannot understand this, that they form coping skills and defense mechanisms to shield themselves as much as possible from this deep-seeded pain. They put up walls of self-protection that can look like: being the class clown, acting like they don't care, deliberate insubordination, social withdrawal, obsessive submersion into an activity, art or sport as avoidance, risqué behavior, over-achieving, to name a few. The coping modality or defense mechanism will be directly correlated to the wound they are attempting to circumvent "feeling or re-living." These wounds become so suppressed that even as adults, we forget we still carry them, and eventually they become our "shadows."

A note here on Ancestral/ Generational Traumas

The terms ancestral and generational trauma can be used interchangeably in the sense that they both refer to trauma that we feel but is not our specific experience. It's trauma that we inherit or is passed down to us genetically. In our specific family lineage or across a generation, there may have been traumatic experiences which led to damaging anguish and suffering across all aspects of life – economic, social, cultural etc. These can include fear, stress, anxiety, depression, anger, hopelessness, and other various mental health afflictions that stem from poverty consciousness, violence, abuse (physical, sexual, verbal), suicide, obesity, addictions etc.

These embedded traumas can be passed down in the family line to the next generation and can play a significant role in creating our own inner child wounds depending upon how heavily they are still embedded in those who raise us. When we take on the wounds of our family lineage, we may feel the emotional weight as if it's our own and develop coping and defense mechanisms accordingly, even if we never experienced the trauma first-hand. This, however, is not a permanent state. The study of epigenetics shows us that in response to such trauma our bodies can alter the gene expression through our awareness, experiences, and choices. We possess the ability to heal ourselves and break this chain.

Let's keep going to see how all of this is healed.

CHAPTER 3

—•◦•—

Patterns and Healing

As we move into adulthood, we take all our shadows with us: our wounds (internalized messages + beliefs) our coping modalities and defense mechanisms (behavior) along with our deep-seeded rejection and abandonment, ancestral traumas, and early familial relationship dynamics. We take these with us "subconsciously" and as stated earlier they will be operating like a computer program in the background directing our life and everything in it. As we grow up, we subconsciously try to heal these wounds through everyone we meet.

Let's go back to our example of Eve. We established how her early social conditioning formed her belief systems, wounds, and behaviors. Her social conditioning also formed her early relational dynamics both male and female. Whichever parent was the one that dispensed the constant criticism in her case study, her relationship with that parent might have proved contentious throughout her childhood, she might have developed repressed anger and resentment if she was not allowed to give voice to her feelings, a lack of trust, respect, and intimacy also may have formed leading to a general emotional disconnect. Moving forward this dynamic with all its triggers and her responses, respectively, will come into focus again, on repeat, in her future relationships with friends, colleagues, lovers/spouses. The purpose of this subconscious repetition is to re-create the childhood dynamic in an attempt to heal it and the wound it created. Crazy? It sure sounds like it, but this is how we try to right the wrong and heal. Each time this dynamic is re-created in a future relationship Eve is given the opportunity to observe and discern what is happening, why, how to neutralize the trigger, and how to change her response, until it is healed. When this dynamic has repeated itself in our adult relationships enough times, we start to notice a *pattern* emerging. This noticing, this awareness of the pattern is where the healing can begin should we choose it.

Patterns are our clue and pointer to where we are harboring shadows that are false and no longer serving us. You can spot a pattern because it will look like the same play, same scene, yet different characters and locales. These will be evident and can happen over a period of months or years depending on how much you are paying attention. The patterns will continue to pop up until we are ready to consciously examine why they exist and where they stem from. Here is where our free will choice comes in. Many people feel "stuck" or stay "stuck" when they either refuse to pay attention and unravel the worn out, non-serving dynamic or when they are afraid to face it head on. Life and our subconscious, however, will keep bringing it to our door until we cannot ignore it anymore. When the pain of standing still holding onto our wounds as they create havoc outweighs the fear of moving forward, we tend to implement the inner work and healing necessary.

When we miss the patterning or deliberately avoid it because we are not yet ready it will intensify to get our attention. A soft tap on the shoulder is a clue that something is amiss, it's an SOS signal when ignored or resisted can turn into discomfort, can turn into a meltdown, and even a full-blown break. We will become aware of this intensification because we will feel afraid, overwhelmed, anxious or even suffer panic attacks. In such instances, we choose to continue living our lives in what we deem "safe mode". We stay in our comfort zones, circumstances that are familiar, we make excuses, deny, rationalize, lie to ourselves, create alternate realities or delusions to live in – anything to avoid touching where it is painful. We choose to stay in lives of limitation based on false beliefs we have held onto. Healing happens when we *incrementally* walk through this pain- unraveling it as situations arise. If we choose to pass on these opportunities, we will continue to re-create them each time with more intensity to nudge us into healing. Conversely, if we choose to be brave and proactive, we can circumvent the repetition of the pattern preventing future suffering.

The Progression of Self-Betrayal, Guilt/ Shame, Self-Punishment, and Self-Sabotage

When we are in fear, resistance or denial of our patterns and the inner child wounds they represent, the manifestation of new feelings and states enter the emotional body and begin to take hold. These specific emotions wreak havoc with our emotional well-being, truly eroding our sense of self. The imprinting of an internalized message remains with us until we prove to ourselves its untrue. Even if we have moved far from our nuclear family, have minimal contact, or they have passed, still the messages remain.

They are no longer being reinforced by those who caused them but by us. We have taken up that task, playing "the tape" of the message over and over on our own. And if we interpreted our messages negatively, we have these additional emotions that come in.

The first is self-betrayal. This is the worst type of betrayal. No other betrayal causes as much pain as self-betrayal, but we rarely perceive this simply because the pain and knowledge that *we* are now the ones perpetuating our own suffering is too much to bear. This pain is so indescribable and incomprehensible that we bury it, so deeply in fact that we forget it exists and live instead from the persona we have created from childhood, societal conditioning, and pre-programmed expectations all the while self-projecting our wounds onto others. The more we do this, the more we consistently continue to compromise ourselves – in our marriage, work, families – and we do this on autopilot.

Every time we lie to ourselves, give ourselves away, cast ourselves aside on a consistent basis, live in self-denial out of fear – fear of being our authentic selves, fear of abandonment or rejection, fear of judgement or criticism, we are betraying ourselves. This constant self-betrayal causes a slow disconnection from our sense of self leading to feelings of guilt and shame. We feel guilt for lacking the courage, ability, and strength to face our wounds and heal them. We feel shame associated with embarrassment and humiliation towards ourselves, feeling innately and wholly bad and wrong. Spiritually, guilt and shame reside and are the lowest forms on the emotional scale and heavy burdens to carry. They are the most detrimental to the self and when left unaddressed morph into many different forms of self-punishment and self-sabotage.

We subconsciously punish ourselves and our familial perpetrators either directly or in the form of others who may portray similar character traits. When left unbridled and unhealed, self-punishment manifests outwardly in all sorts of ways, some more sublime than others, that are very detrimental and hurtful to us and others. It can take many forms such as: a constant denial of pleasurable activities, or a non-existent social life or superficial friends, to toxic relationships, sexual behaviors of punishment such as bondage etc. Self-punishment says, "I have to pay a price for everything I want." In short, anything or anyone who demonstrates compassion, truth, self-love, and forgiveness is kept at a distance so we can keep re-creating our self-fulfilling prophecy cycle. We feel guilty and "bad" (shame) and so we keep acting out as such and associating with people and circumstances who keep us "stuck" in this belief, to prove ourselves right.

Likewise, self-sabotage has the same effect and is associated with low self-worth/self-esteem. When we engage in self-sabotage, we are preventing ourselves from doing what we desire to do, from reaching our goals. This behavior stems from the "I don't deserve" belief system. Self-sabotage can be sublime and present itself in the milder forms of procrastination, stress eating, chronic lateness, intimacy, and commitment issues, for example or more serious forms such as risqué sexual behavior or addiction. Self-sabotage in and of itself creates patterns that can be traced back to our unaddressed inner child wounds and patterns. Self-sacrifice is one of these patterns.

Self-sacrifice as a self-sabotaging behavior puts us in a perceived state of martyrdom, believing that when we give up something for someone else, we will feel "good" about ourselves and in turn receive love, affection, recognition, accolades etc. It's used to combat the underlying belief that says, "we are not good enough". However, this is a boomerang because martyrdom is not valued the way we think it is. The accolades or recognition we might receive will be indifferent or fleeting, but not consistent – people move on quickly – and constant martyrdom breeds resentment in yourself and others.

When does this cycle of behaviors stemming from guilt and shame stop? When our repetitive patterns begin to bring into our awareness the knowledge that what we are continuing to do to ourselves is far worse than whatever the original wound was. Once this glimmer of truth is perceived we can begin the work of healing the original wound. There are no short-cuts in emotional work, everything keeps bringing us back to healing the original wounds. This is the goal, everything else is a band aid.

Self-Protection

Another simultaneous facet of the inner child wounds is the building of inner walls of self-protection. This wall was subconsciously created in childhood to protect us from feeling the pain, suffering and heartbreak of these wounds. The goal of the wall at all costs is to keep us from experiencing them again. This is where our false ego derived from our human identity comes into play. Its job is to keep us "safe." It does not distinguish what we define as "safe". It only knows when fear is expressed within the body and mind it will do its job to build walls of self-protection and fight to keep them there. In attempting to keep out any future potential experiences that could trigger the old pain, it also inadvertently keeps out love.

However, a wounded/ broken heart is merely a heart that is a little more open and underneath the pain lies the desire for more love to be felt and received. When we freeze out love due to fear of vulnerability, we block ourselves from receiving, feeling, and living out the very healing, life and love we desire. This wall creates pain in and of itself, in addition to our wounds. When we were small children, this wall served a purpose as we were dependent, but as we move into adulthood it becomes an obstacle. Pain is an inevitable part of evolution. It is through painful experiences that we learn our greatest lessons about who we are and it's the driving force behind our choice to heal and move forward. Suffering, on the other hand, is temporary and perpetuates when we do not perceive the pain as the gift and the prompt to healing and release. Suffering locks down guilt/shame and resistance keeping you stuck. There is nothing enlightening about suffering when it is not used to propel you into awareness, healing, and evolution.

As much as you're hurting, try to step into the position of an observant witness to see what this experience is teaching you about who you are. Sit still and do some breath work and allow the truth of the experience to reveal itself. Remember the pain is only a conduit to a greater "**inner**standing" and suffering is just your default response, perception, and thoughts about what transpired. Focus on the incredible capacity of love that lives within your heart and being and allow it to carry you forward and out of your wounded cycle.

Healing Patterns - Observation and Discernment – Bearing Witness Technique

Healing is a challenging and incremental process. The wounds, beliefs, and behaviors we have internalized and have been carrying around for years cannot be healed overnight. One effective technique to integrate is that of observation and discernment. It requires us to move into a *neutral* state and observe ourselves as if we were an impartial witness. See if you can suspend your emotional response to your wounds, or the specific situation at hand, long enough for you to move into observation mode. This neutral space will afford you clarity and discernment. By bearing witness you can discern what is truly happening beyond the emotional response of pain and suffering. You can see where you are in guilt or shame and what your patterns are. From there you can trace back to the origins of the belief system you carry and where and when you internalized an inaccurate message about who you are.

As you trace back and begin pulling apart your shadows, ask yourself: is this belief I am carrying true? Where did this originate from? How did I internalize it? How am I re-creating this dynamic and belief? What do I truly believe about who I am? Who am I beyond who I was told I was?

When doing this, turn your brain off (breathing techniques assist with this) as you are not seeking your opinion, or an intellectual response based on your memory bank data. Instead, move into a space of silence and stillness. Silence allows the mind to get quiet and stillness allows the body to move into a relaxed (uncontracted) state. When you ask the questions feel into your body. Is there a reaction and if so, where? What does it feel like? The body never lies but you must learn to discern your body's response accurately. This takes practice but eventually you will be able to distinguish truth from fiction. Here are some markers to help. Fiction feels like anxiety, panic, uneasiness, nervousness, contraction, while truth will feel like calmness, alignment, peace, and clarity.

As you do this work, *do not* compare your wounds to those of others- it's not a contest as to who had it worse, it's all relative. The more you keep talking about it in this way the more it remains in and becomes your identity. You don't want to stay in this space. As you unravel and heal your shadows, your authentic self-identity will start to take form and your human and spiritual identity will come into harmony and alignment.

Spiritual Perspective on Shadow Healing

Our soul and divine self are always presenting us with opportunities to heal, evolve and course correct. To heal and release all our wounds so that we may continue to step into who we truly are. One of the ways it does this is by using these patterns along with the accompanying challenges, obstacles, and difficulties, to stimulate our awareness so we may begin to exercise our free will choice to do the inner work of healing. Some of us need to have quite challenging circumstances to implement shifts while others do not. This depends on how willing we are to commit to ourselves and to embrace the healing and lesson our pattern is there to teach us.

What is the purpose of the pattern from this perspective? Our divine self and divine source continually work to push us to decode and heal our inner childhood wounds to teach us, consciously and experientially, to make a free will choice to return and re-embrace the state we once knew and have forgotten. To bring us back into our organic state, our inner wisdom and awareness that we are eternal spiritual beings; whole and complete, loving and loveable, and that the purpose of our human identity is to live out *this* truth, not the identity our limited human culture would have us believe. To bring us back to our own self-love.

If we allow, by free will choice, the mind (our logic and intellect), to override the signal from our spirit aspect (divine self) we are in essence spiritually bypassing and will remain out of alignment. Remember from Book 1 we defined alignment as the human trifecta of mind body spirit existing in authentic truth and expressing this truth as a harmonized integrated whole. Our divine self in conjunction with our divine source always wants to bring us back into our natural state of true self-love and authenticity. Bypassing causes our wounds to remain and our patterns to come around again, stronger, until we are willing to grasp this truth. This is not a punishment but an experiential teaching of self-love to propel growth and evolution.

A note here on the Universal Law of Attraction. I add this here for clarification purposes as mainstream media has misinterpreted its function and uses it to bypass doing the inner work of healing and self-love. In very simple terms the Law states "like attracts like," no exceptions. This means we attract what *we are*, not what *we want* no matter how many affirmations or visualizations we do. Translated, it means we attract from our inner state of who we believe we are and what we truly feel we deserve. If subconsciously we truly believe, we don't deserve or are unworthy etc. we will inevitably draw to us situations or persons that will *ultimately* reflect those beliefs back to us in some way, even if at the beginning that circumstance or person seemed like what we had been asking for. This is called *mirroring*. There is no bypassing Spirit and Universal Laws. We must look at our underlying programming. Spirit gifts us with intuition and is always present to guide us along. It's our job to listen and pull it out from under the rug and make the "free will choice" to put in the inner work - heal and evolve. The Law, when used as intended, helps us to see where we are at internally by what is happening to us externally. Remember "as within, so without."

CHAPTER 4

———•❖•———

Learning Unconditional Self-Love

To recap we learned how our self-love is innate and became dimmed and obstructed by the formations of our childhood wounds, brought on from adapting to life in our human nuclear family, community, and society. We learned that we internalized these wounds in a way that was inaccurate and detrimental to our core being. We learned these wounds created belief systems and subsequent behaviors that formed patterns and inner walls and when denied created self-defeating and self-sabotaging emotions. We learned that true self-love is an ongoing lifelong incremental process of unraveling these wounds and returning to our true spiritual identity and the inner state it creates. We learned the fundamental components of self-love; radical honesty, acknowledgement and self-knowledge, radical self-acceptance, self-trust, self-forgiveness, and self-care as tangible guides to reclaiming and returning to self-love.

Here we put it all together, with some strategies to help us along, to understand what unconditional authentic self-love looks like. Even though we seem to "forget" our authentic identity as we move through our human life our spiritual identity is never truly forgotten but rather suppressed under the surface of our busy human lives. It is always present, tapping us on the shoulder with gentle guidance. There is always that underlying sense of its presence throughout our life. We are just not focused on it; therefore, we do not perceive it.

It is vital in this process of returning to our self-love that we employ courage, compassion, kindness, and to give ourselves grace. We tend to be much more forgiving and tenderer with others than with ourselves. Remember, the process moves incrementally so we do not short-circuit ourselves while unraveling our wounds and retrieving all our perceived broken parts and fragmentation. The goal is to heal and release and this takes time. We work one layer at a time, going deeper each time and allowing for integration in-between. Evolution and growth are a life-long process. This does not mean it is always painful but will be joyous as well, as you keep elevating.

This process is also a "solo" process for the most part. As much as we might desire to share it with others (therapists excluded), we open ourselves up to receiving commentary and opinions from both well-meaning and ill-intentioned friends and family who are on a different journey, having different experiences and different lessons. They will dispense advice based on that which might not be relevant or in resonance with ours. We must discern what we share and where it is appropriate and beneficial. The only person keeping you from loving yourself is, in fact, you. This is your inner work, not theirs. Ultimately, there should be no human head above your own in this process, no matter their rank, title, position, or status. **No-one else knows your full journey and what is best for you other than you, and no-one outside of you will love you more than you are willing to love yourself. As long as you hold a place within you wherein you do not love yourself, you will always, without exception, see it reflected back (mirrored) to you by someone in your life. The lesson is always there.**

When our self-love is secure and grounded, we will never be coerced or influenced by anyone external to us. We are all defined by our free will choices. As much as we want to blame others for the choices we make, we alone are responsible and accountable for what we choose and create. When there is no sense of self or self-love, we give our power away and are easily influenced to follow others. Living in today's materialistic world has caused humanity to base their sense of self on transient things and to extrapolate our worthiness from these same transient things keeping our inner state just as transient as opposed to grounded, centered and solidified. Self-love gives us a foundational sense of self that cannot be shaken rendering us empowered in our lives and its decisions and direction. The key here is to keep going within for our own guidance.

Accessing our Spiritual Identity/Divine Self

Our personal wisdom comes from our experiences and from within. Guidance and support on this journey come from accessing our divine self and divine source. It is from our spiritual identity that further wisdom and clarity is imparted. Learn to start an on-going conversation with this aspect of yourself and make it a practice to keep connecting there. Sit in the silence and stillness as mentioned above. For it is in this state that you are accessing your spiritual aspect. Set your intentions, ask your questions and trust that the answers will be shown to you with clarity, in proper timing. You are not alone, but also in the hands of the divine, co-creating (see Book 1).

When we are embodying unconditional self-love and self-worth, we come into wholeness and oneness, both within ourselves and with others; for it leads us right into our heart space. It is through our heart center that we access and experience love and our divine self and source. Connecting with our heart is a key practice. As we continue to develop and embrace unconditional self-love, we will organically embody all the qualities of our true spiritual being and these include all "the virtues" - authenticity, truth, justice, integrity, honesty, compassion and so on. For love eradicates fear, distortion, and chaos. Self-love not only heals you but empowers and restores you.

The State of Neutrality

Learning to practice "neutrality" is the gift spirit affords and teaches us to use on this journey back home to ourselves. For spirit resides in love and neutrality. As discussed earlier in our observation/discernment technique, maintaining a state of neutrality as we move on our evolutionary journey keeps us from triggering and allows for clarity in all circumstances. It allows us to manage healing and change more effectively, bringing us into a state of balance. Most of humanity is resistant to change because they are afraid and have not been taught that change and Love is the only constant in the universe. Change makes us feel unsafe. Humanity has learned *fear* and fear wishes to control all things in the name of self-protection. Fear is an illusion of human conditioning. It does not keep us safe, as we believe, but rather completely closed off, paralyzed and hypervigilant. Love and fear cannot co-exist in the same space. Therefore, we must trust and make a choice. This choice gets easier the more we practice self-love and the more connected we are to our divine self and source.

A wonderful mantra to embrace here: *"Show me Spirit, beyond words...show me who I am, fill me with the light and love that I remember and seems lost. Break open my wounds and their wall of protection to help me open to the love within me and around me."*

Remember, our desire for unconditional love, acceptance, joy, bliss begins with us and within us. It is the calling back home to love from Spirit to our natural state of being and our innate spiritual nature. We are about the business of evolution and setting ourselves free. This is our purpose and the journey, and this is what it means "to know thyself".

Here are a few more techniques to help you along the way.

CHAPTER 5

More Strategies to Help you Along

Keep a diary – A diary is different than a journal. Keeping a written diary of your experiences, feelings, awareness', questions, progress, and healing as it occurs gives you a quick timeline and allows you to capture an experience and your thoughts in the moment. This is a short-form notation that you can circle back to in-depth, later, in your journal. Keeping the diary on you is key.

Journal – Journaling is a long-form examination of what was noted in your diary. Here you can explore all the above and draw your conclusions. Here you should ask the following questions to give you structure and keep you focused on self-love as the goal. Apply to each situation.

o   Where am I not loving and accepting myself?

o   Where am I not trusting myself?

o   Where am I abandoning/rejecting myself?

o   What belief system is being expressed?

o   Was I self-projecting, coming from my inner child wounds?

o   What was reflected back to me?

Perceive everything as a teaching and not an attack – Even though you might be hurt, choose to see every interaction or situation wherein you are triggered as a teaching and not an attack. This will neutralize your reactive response and give you the pause and opportunity *to choose* your response in the moment. Later, you can reflect on why you were triggered and what you learned about yourself from the interaction.

Practice non-judgment towards yourself – different from observation/discernment vs. judgment/criticism as discussed earlier and applied to others. Here we must understand that self-development, growth, and evolution take time. Understand it's a process and where you are in any given moment is exactly where you are supposed to be – there is no right or wrong in the process itself. Sometimes it's one step forward, two back and at other times it's a leap then a status quo for a time. Go with the flow of it, maintaining conscious awareness. It's a cyclical process, not linear. Judging your process is self-defeating.

Suspend expectations – it is crucial to not only suspend your expectations of the timeline of your process and your "performance" but also to suspend your expectations from others to give you what you need and towards yourself from needing it from them.

Re-introduce yourself to yourself – give yourself the mental and physical space to allow who you are authentically to rise to the surface organically. Suspend all your belief systems, labels, and thoughts about who you are, as much as possible to allow new information emerge.

Time alone – do not be afraid to spend time alone and on activities, trips, or at home in a solo capacity. You cannot hear yourself when you're busy listening to outside noise. You don't have to go along with others if it does not resonate with you or if you want to be alone. You do not need to seek another's permission or approval for this. When you're home dispense with filling your hours in front of the TV, instead, engage in a creative artistic pursuit such as art, music, creative cooking, gardening etc. as these "inspirations" come directly from Spirit.

Meditate/Stillness/Silence – make a choice to consciously spend time each day sitting in silence, stillness, or meditation. Here is where you will connect and hear the voice of your divine self and source. Contemplation and reflection allow for clarity and guidance.

Engage in movement and inspired activities – move your body in whatever way it's feeling inclined to in the moment. Step away from organized exercises, repetitive routines, specific music, and forms of exercise. Give your body the opportunity to express itself naturally – listen to what it needs. Moving the lymphatic system in conjunction with moving your spirit, while suspending your mental mind promotes a more complete sense of release and freedom from stuck emotions leading to a complete reset in that moment.

Return to childhood innocence – Be silly, play, do nothing, sleep with your favorite stuffed animal, make a snowman, put on skates and go around the block, ride your bike as you did when you were a kid - carefree, hug someone just because, laugh long and in full self-expression unique to you, spend time alone exploring the woods, the beach, paying attention to those surroundings while turning off your mind and its endless desire to categorize, label, assess, and overthink. Engaging in child-like activities re-connects us to the inner child, its purity and innocence. It allows the inner child an opportunity to emerge and as he/she blends with us, fostering healing.

Mirror Therapy – Spend time really looking at yourself in the mirror beyond your physical appearance. Try to see the soul behind your eyes, the beauty of the function of your body and what a beautiful tool and gift it is to live your life. Look at who you are within and note what is reflected to you. Appreciate and send love to every part of who you are.

Gratitude - Honor every step of this journey, every tear, every cry of anguish, every moment of anger or bitterness or pain. Honor every part of who you are and where you are in this process. You are not here by accident. Gratitude is tangible and the process becomes easier when we understand it is a gift to bring you back home to loving yourself.

Therapy – Seek out professional help if needed. There is no stigma to having unbiased support to help you through the more challenging healing.

Comprehension of Purpose – Understanding that this process is all for the purpose of spiritual and human evolution allows you to embrace the journey easier. It gives meaning to why you experience what you do. Understand that loving yourself is how you set yourself free from the emotional chains that bind you, your perceived limitations as defined by another, and moves you out of internal conflict and into peace and elevation.

Epilogue

"Self-love can be described as rite of passage, if you will, for it is the road into wholeness and oneness from within one's consciousness. Everyone is on a different path and at a different point on their path. There is no right or wrong, or comparison's to be made here. As each soul journeys onward through lifetime after lifetime, they will come to different levels of self-love. It is not necessarily something that is accomplished in one lifetime but can be approached in a multi-faceted way. It is indeed an honor to walk this path although from the human perspective it is not perceived as such, but this is the purpose of incarnation for as we learn, and as we evolve, we learn the path of self-love and we walk the path of self-love. Coming into wholeness may span many lifetimes and this is the work of each soul and with each incarnation, amongst

other reasons. Be heartened and know that this is the purpose for which humanity has come.

As you learn to go within you will find through your heart center...there will reside the love that you seek and the love of Spirit. There is your connection to what you would call your home and there is where you will find us. But it is a choice and a decision for you to come and seek us, for we are always there waiting for you to make that choice.

It is necessary on each of your journeys, through each of your lifetimes, that you have contrast, for it is within the contrast that you learn and have the most growth. This is the road and the path and should be embraced from this perspective. Do not be afraid to look at the contrast, for it is through the darkness that you find your light...and through the light that you return to self-love, to wholeness and oneness."

May you all be blessed.

Anthony

Preamble on Book Three in the Human Case of Mistaken Identity Series

Relationships as a Teaching Tool

What is it that makes some relationships so loving while others so contentious?

The masculine and feminine have suffered under stereotypes for millennia. The dynamic between the two and the true spiritual essence and meaning have become distorted and abused to suit the human agenda and the struggle for control and power. However, the masculine and feminine is an eternal dance of true partnership and oneness. In Book Three we will explore the masculine/feminine and its different forms of relationships from a completely different perspective. What they are here to teach us about who we are and how to perceive each other.